Just Last Days

Just Last Days

Poems by Mark Robinson

Published by WordTech Editions

P.O. Box 541106

Cincinnati, OH 45254-1106

ISBN: 978-1-62549-338-5

Poetry Editor: Kevin Walzer

Business Editor: Lori Jareo

Visit us on the web at www.wordtechweb.com

Previously published:

Letter in Di-vers-ity: Austin International Poetry Festival Anthology
Tumor in Bending Genres
Invisible in Red Flag Poetry Postcard Series
Ask in Naugatuck River Review
Mountainside in September in Levee Magazine
Every Door in Riza Press Journal
Wrong Sky and *Spring Chrysalis* in Exterminated Angel Press: The Magazine

Contents

Something Simple

I wish that something simple
would come to me

like a small child
placing a square
of chocolate

on his tongue,
it's sweetness saying

this is how it is
and
this is how we should say it is.

Night

Darkening, darkening, darkening
night. I take my sleep like a drowning
diver: sighing, sinking, choking.

My daughter accepts it like
only a child can. Using my belly
to rest her head, then the crook

where my knee bends, before
finally resting, her head
on my shoulder, her mouth to my ear

as if waiting, trying to remember
a secret she was making up.
The breeze lifts through green tender

leaves, an exhale, her defeated sigh,
whisper suspended in the darkening night.

Imagination at Midnight

I.

That white-blossoming
wonder might be an apple tree
if not for the absence of the sweet fruit.

In any case, its brilliance
lasts only an hour every April
before its petals are spring's first vagabonds
and the softer flora of summer takes its place.

II.

Sometimes after dusk, I wonder
how long it took a seedling
to fall into the neighbor's yard,

grab hold of the wet soil
and burst wildly upward.

Its uppermost branches fasten to the wind—-
a never-before voice,
present and inquisitive,

breathing midnight's echo
night after night after night.

III.

Two evergreens in the backyard,
bride and groom, side by side,
the taller one on the right, watching

nobly over his partner. Together
they are a single dark silhouette,
combining to break up the sky

roots intertwined,
married to nightfall.

The Motion Of Being

Music, we born forget,
Is a streaming rhythm, a beating flood
A waterfall of flowing blood
From a larger heart.

Eyes unopened, breath unformed
But limbs, in fluid...move
That dance— there must be dancing!
Still buried in the womb.

Wrong Sky

Verse, like a cat, paws at the door
trying to find a loose thread
in the fabric of time

A place to slip out
and into the world.

Tonight, that rare blood-orange
moon, neglected disc of wisdom.

Me, trying to plot the coordinates
of my dreams, looking in the wrong sky
night after night.

Mountainside in September

Up here you can catch
at just that delicate moment
the perfect brilliance of bright yellow Aspen leaves
dotting the deep evergreen mountainside.

In a long white coat, a faceless surgeon
explains the fiery spotting on a scan of my lungs
and a plan for numbing my body
enough to cut into the healthy flesh
to remove the ravishing pits.

My chest glowing coals, I celebrate those colors
that overtake summer's shiny green leaves:
the yellows, the oranges
and the reds that must drop soon
lest their fluid freeze
damaging them beyond use.

I Am

Somewhere, tonight. The world rotates uncontrollably.
Wolves sing at the moon; the mountain lions, their eyes
dance
on the city lights, each distant and measured
and bright. The sky is its own music
without form or boundary, a starry composition:
a twinkling song that sings of who I am.

Everything is telling me to speak of who I am.
The world around me shudders uncontrollably:
it will not be contained by the black notes of composition.
Clouds float like smoke, a sky-dance
happening each night with the music
coming from above, and within, that cannot be measured.

What takes place when your frozen breath is measured
in heartbeats? With weakened voice I am
singing a disjointed song. Just more divine music
bursting forth and inside I cry uncontrollably
in the vast night while the dark dance continues
close overhead— a moving push-pin composition.

Even then it is *my* composition:
a story breaking open, falsely measured
in pages, or lines, or even the words that dance
back and forth and fall from the sky. I am
reminded the truth is always told, often uncontrollably,
unleashed after years of shadowed music

kept hidden. Each voice has its own music
and melody, its secret composition
either kept, or better yet, escaping uncontrollably
like a woman's labor measured

in hours and minutes. The new life, I am
certain, should always be celebrated in dance.

Praying on a star that burns out in its dance
through nothingness, friction is music
and the flashing brilliance reminds me that *I am.*
Living luminaries perch brightly on a black composition
that somewhere, somehow is always measured
exactly. In the distance, the wind sings uncontrollably.

Even now, the music that springs from composition
leaps like a life-giving dance, a measured
rhythm. In my sky, I am blooming uncontrollably.

Ask

Watching you waddle
through the crowd to our resting
spot in the grass beneath the oak tree

after taking down the Memphis Totchos
for the third day in a row

is like watching a wounded bull
stumbling to find his safe spot in the inescapable ring.
Can we come again next year?

Who thought to put bananas and peanut sauce
on top of tater tots and bacon?

and

Who brought this small child
who thinks all the world exquisite?

Later in the dairy building
we stand in wonderment at *The Last Supper*
chiseled in grade A butter.

The long hair of Jesus is bright yellow.
I will never eat butter again.

Peter is there, and Judas,
and the rest. But I do not recognize
their polished faces.

I imagine the bread at this meal
is creamy and sweet.

The wine, smooth.
It this was the last time Jesus ate
why didn't he have a glo-cone for dessert?

Do you have any more questions?
There is more: *ask*.

Hush

I want to see deer again
there in the woods
on the trail where we stopped:
spirited creatures

in the movement of the day
in the arrangement of the universe
perceive us watching
and interrupt that dance.

The larger one raises a curious
nose in the air,
slick black eyes asking
Why have you come?

Wind gathers in the distance,
rolling through treetops
like the ocean

swallowing every sound
until the deer rush off
leaving us alone

in that hush of waves,
asking ourselves
Why have we come?

Instructions for Buying Avocados

If they are a dollar and nineteen,
buy three, the unripe and overly firm.

I like to see the bright green
lined up on the kitchen counter
before they turn dark and soften.

If they are eighty-nine cents apiece
please buy four,
but if by chance they are sixty-nine cents
always get five.

Anything less than that
drop to your knees
(on this be vigilant)

and praise the divine
for this gift—let the bag overflow.
Avocados are, we know,
the fruit of angels.

Finally, do not forget to take a picture
with your phone
so later we can post it on Facebook

and share this
good news.

Every Door

Every door is married
to the idea of *the other side,*
and opens to a mystery.
How many times,

buried in the slight
crack at the bottom of
a coffee cup do I
search for you?

In sleep
our hands embrace
like Miller's knot tied
around an ancient
burlap sack of rice.

Your heart has two doors:
the door called *faith*
and the door you emerge from
when you awake, that stirs

again my searching.
If your hand un-hands from mine,
as if engraved into my palm
I take it with me, that ghost-hand.

Spring Chrysalis

We talk about the weather often,
how cold it is here this morning,
every morning.
And how it should be snowing, but it isn't.

Bleakness, be my guide:
these poems need us.
Without our voices, yours and mine,
the world is nothing more than milky images,
as if squinting at the moon.

If not through us, how can any song enter the universe?

Our words shape the gray florid clouds,
the patterns in the cliff side,
the structure of a snowflake.

We will remember this colorless season

and when we spin our spring chrysalis,
it will become transparent
revealing the brilliant inside.

Tumor

Great bright peach burning
in my throat. You smother
my voice, feed off my breath,
turning and revolting
against me. I would rather

jab a knife and swallow blood
than lie on my back
day after day under that mesh mask.
The hood of silence hovers
over me and at last

that blister roasting has melted to pitiful nothing.
Listen,

after all that flesh lost
I am too frail even for bathing. Clouded
with an ether of the most

basic bodily quest to keep the heart
thumping, thumping, thumping like a sick hammer
inside. The repeating
of its simple report:

How quickly,
how quickly we do go through this life.

Pantoum

We two gather twelve eggs
from our cackling hens
drawing them into the gut of our lives.
One by one, eleven shells crack.

With the last unbroken,
we carry a dozen eggs
across the earthen floor
into the center of the universe.

Outside, our hens— they laugh hideously.
We consider our single egg, unceremoniously.
One by one, each bone shatters,
my rib cage surrounding a thousand confessions.

Without grief, we study our last egg,
barefoot on the unforgiving kitchen floor.
Listen, inside my chest is a city of hearts,
one left unbroken.

The Invisible

Lately, I have been longing
for fog. Say, the morning
considers sleeping a little longer
and a misty curtain refuses to rise.

When the invisible
calls, how should we answer?

Three times
my mother said
no thank you.

Others gave that voice
a body promptly.

In time we will know
the secrets of the saints
and of the monks
walking through the mist,

water droplets hanging in the air,
their craving long-
since fulfilled.

Letter

When your letter arrived
I held the envelope in my hands
as if it were your hands,

Studied its circular cursive:
your name, my name,
the names of our distant cities…

how you slipped from me
into those round, looping letters.

Where Birds Live

Outside my window
attached to the tree
a blue birdhouse,
the black roof and open doorway,
imperfect in shape.

Are birds indifferent to where they reside?

Consider the scraps
scraped together in the high bare trees—
mud, mangled twigs, moss, feathers,
the soft hair of your mother
all part of a bowl-shaped nest.

Exposed and content
chirping earnestly at sunrise
making every garden a reckless possibility
of awakening to the world—
they neither sow, nor reap, nor gather into barns.

How simple they live in this shining moment,
how complex their instincts to survive.

Raindrops slide rapidly down my window,
the birdhouse secure on the trunk of the tree.

Solitaire

Each morning the sun casts shade on the clapboard
buildings opposite a man walking alone
on the clean and empty sidewalk.
From here, he doesn't need a map.

Up and over the hill where the bare branches
        of the elms and
        of the oaks
spread out like cracks in the glassy blue sky.

Once I was this man,
stopping next to a crumbling silo
to light a cigarette,
in my chest a concrete heart.

He continues. His dark shadow,
        the dark shadows of the trees,
        of the tiny box-shaped houses
form a silhouette beautiful and humble in its decay.

Inis Mór

Above, the deep gray, ever-
shifting Irish sky listens:
white waves plunge against

the exposed and ancient cliff.
It's so quiet in the world.

Lying on my belly, inching forward
to look over the precipice:
the wild earth rises straight up

from nowhere.
Below the untamed surf beckons
and for just a moment, I want

to merge with that rage,
to fall over and into it.

Dear Mr. Stevens

Here the birds sound like howling dogs
in the middle of the day
in the middle of the desert.
At night words like *feather* and *fluttering*
fill my dreams.
There is something harsh
about the front lawns of pebbles and sand
but the pale moon hangs large over downtown
in constant morning sun.
The pastel yellow plaster of the Roman church,
its beautifully manicured and deep green grass
stands out as the sort of haven
you would have searched out in this dusty town.
Alone in the darkness, in a pew
among the candles and the crucifix,
your face still and your eyes closed
wrestling to reconcile the real with the imagined
arranging, deepening, enchanting
never hearing the pounding on the door,
the crowd of us frantic to get in.

Made in the USA
Monee, IL
20 January 2020

20550017R00021